STUDY GUIDE

Why We Trust the Bible

Stephen J. Nichols

LIGONIER MINISTRIES
Renew your Mind.
LIGONIER.ORG | 800-435-4343

421 Ligonier Court, Sanford, FL 32771
Email: info@ligonier.org

Printed in China.

1

Revelation—Where Would We Be Without It?

MESSAGE INTRODUCTION

Romans 1:19–21 states, "For what can be known about God is plain to them, because God has shown it to them. For his invisible attributes, namely, his eternal power and divine nature, have been clearly perceived, ever since the creation of the world, in the things that have been made. So they are without excuse." Paul writes these words to demonstrate, among other things, the nature of revelation and the benefits and demands flowing from it. All men witness the glory of God and owe Him allegiance, for the oceans, mountains, and forests attest to His existence and authority as much as the consciousness that absorbs and categorizes these experiences. No man possesses excuse. Nonetheless, he proceeds to explain that this revelation, known as general revelation, does not lead to salvation, for sin has corrupted man's ability to acknowledge the Lord as God. Thus, the Lord revealed Himself to man directly and specifically, culminating in the revelation of Jesus Christ. Through Christ, God's plan to redeem a remnant for Himself climaxed, and the doctrine of Scripture, the topic of this series, describes and analyzes the written work detailing God's initiative to redeem the world—a work sufficient for the life of His followers.

SCRIPTURE READINGS

Psalm 19; 1 Thessalonians 2:13; John 6:66–69; Acts 17; Romans 1

TEACHING OBJECTIVES

1. To introduce and analyze two texts of Scripture that will form the framework for this series on the doctrine of Scripture.
2. To describe the doctrine of revelation, general and special, as well as to list the attributes of revelation

QUOTATION

After Darkness, Light.

—A motto of the Protestant Reformation

LECTURE OUTLINE

I. Scripture on the Doctrine of Scripture
   A. Many passages of Scripture provide insight on the doctrine of revelation, but examinations of two texts will suffice in this study to form a framework for the entire series.
      i. 1 Thessalonians 2:13
         1. Paul writes to the church at Thessalonica, a body of believers of which he has fond memories.
         2. With these joyful times in mind, Paul, under the inspiration of the Holy Spirit, writes, "And we also thank God constantly for this. That when you received the Word of God, which you heard from us, you accepted it. Not as the word of men, but as what it really is, the Word of God, which is at work in you believers."
         3. A number of observations arise.
            a. Paul preached the Word to the Thessalonians, and this verse demonstrates that preaching and proclamation are crucial to regeneration and the Christian life.
            b. Most importantly, Paul identified the message that went forth from him as the Word of God.
            c. Paul noted that the Word of God was at work in the Thessalonian believers, transforming them as it took seed and grew within them.
         4. This passage demonstrates that the Word of God is communicated, preached, and proclaimed; it is, in fact, the very Word of God; and it transforms believers into the image of Christ.
      ii. John 6:66–69
         1. After declaring that eternal life hinges on feeding on His body and blood, Jesus witnessed many of His disciples depart on account of this hard saying.
         2. John recounts the interchange that followed: "So Jesus said to the Twelve, 'Do you want to go away as well?' Simon Peter answered him, 'Lord, to whom shall we go? You have the words of eternal life, and we have believed, and have come to know, that you are the Holy One of God.'"
            a. Peter acknowledged that if they did not follow Jesus—as many throughout history have chosen not to do—they would take up some other path or direction.

   b. Peter understood and vocalized that another direction would prove futile, as the words of eternal life sprang from the lips of Jesus alone.

II. The Doctrine of Revelation
- A. Theologians divide revelation into two categories.
  - i. The word "revelation" comes from the Greek word *apokalupsis*, which means, "to take off the cover."
  - ii. The first category is general revelation, the revelation accessible to all mankind through which God reveals His existence and His activity of creating and sustaining all things.
    1. General revelation may be understood in four particular ways.
       - a. God reveals Himself in nature on the whole.
       - b. God reveals Himself in the laws that govern nature.
       - c. God reveals Himself in the harmonious structure of the human body.
       - d. God reveals Himself in the aspects of humanity that transcend physical explanation.
    2. Scripture attests to general revelation in many places, such as Psalm 19, Acts 17, and Romans 1.
  - iii. The second category is special revelation (a.k.a. particular revelation), the revelation by which God speaks directly and specifically.
    1. God has spoken directly and specifically in multiple ways throughout the history of redemption.
    2. Special revelation has culminated in the sixty-six books of the Bible, which point to Jesus as the Christ.

III. Revelation possesses a number of attributes (e.g. what revelation intends to convey).
- A. Necessity: we need general revelation (nature) to reveal the existence of God the creator and special revelation (Scripture) to unveil God as the Redeemer.
- B. Authority: revelation possesses authority over us by virtue of its proclamation from the author of all things.
- C. Clarity (a.k.a. perspicuity): revelation is clear, even if at times difficult to understand.
- D. Sufficiency: revelation is sufficient for all of life.
- E. Beauty: revelation, both nature and Scripture, are beautiful and consistent with the beauty of God.

STUDY QUESTIONS

1. Insights into the doctrine of revelation occur in a few places only, which contributes to an unclear understanding of God's revelation to humanity.
   - a. True
   - b. False

2. In 1 Thessalonians 2:13, Paul explained to the Thessalonians that his preaching originated in himself and he took an educated guess at the will of the Lord for their lives.
   a. True
   b. False

3. In response to Jesus' inquiry to His disciples in John 6:66–69, this disciple declared that eternal life sprang from Jesus' lips.
   a. Thomas
   b. John
   c. James
   d. Peter

4. The word "revelation" comes from the Greek word *apokalupsis*, which means, ____________.
   a. "to take off the cover"
   b. "end times"
   c. "final matters"
   d. "a majestic vision"

5. General revelation is the revelation accessible to all mankind through which God reveals His existence and His activity of creating and sustaining all things.
   a. True
   b. False

BIBLE STUDY AND DISCUSSION QUESTIONS

1. Read 1 Thessalonians 2:13. What do Paul's words convey about his experience in Thessalonica? What does the passage demonstrate about the doctrine of revelation in terms of its communication, origin, and its effects?

2. Read John 6:66–69. What does Peter reveal about Jesus? What do Jesus' words guarantee for those who accept them?

3. What is general revelation? Describe the four particular ways in which general revelation may be understood. Read and discuss some passages of Scripture that attest to general revelation.

4. What is special revelation? What is the culmination of special revelation in redemptive history, and to whom does it point?

5. List and describe the attributes of revelation.

2

The Authority of Scripture, Part 1—The Doctrine of Inspiration

MESSAGE INTRODUCTION

Higher criticism, the branch of literary investigation that seeks to discover the world behind the text, rose to prominence in seventeenth-century Germany. Yet, the motivation for the implementation of this form of study, the denial of biblical inspiration and inerrancy, has a much longer history. Human beings have tried to deny the inspiration of God's Word for ages because they cannot abide God's authority over them. As today's lesson demonstrates, the origin of Scripture in God necessitates its authority over all creation, and only two responses may follow: Spirit-inspired acceptance or denial.

SCRIPTURE READINGS

2 Timothy 3:16–17; 2 Peter 1:16–21

TEACHING OBJECTIVES

1. To explain the origin of Scripture and the nature of authority that its origination institutes
2. To describe the modernistic attitude toward the Bible
3. To demonstrate the harmony between divine inspiration and human authorship

QUOTATION

The Bible is authoritative, for it is the Word of God; it is intelligible, for it is the word of man. Because it is the word of man in every part and element, it comes home to our hearts. Because it is the word of God in every part and element, it is our constant law and guide.

—B.B. Warfield

LECTURE OUTLINE

I. The Doctrine of Inspiration
   A. The word "inspired" comes from 2 Timothy 3:16 (Greek: *theopneustos*, literally "God-breathed").
      i. 2 Timothy 3:16–17: "All Scripture is breathed out by God, and profitable for teaching, for reproof, for correction, for training in righteousness, that the man of God may be competent, equipped for every good work."
      ii. Many biblical texts emphasize the origin of Scripture from God, and this demonstrates that the authority of Scripture comes from "top-down."
         1. The authority of Scripture begins with the Lord and proceeds from his ultimate position of authority.
         2. This truth differentiates Christianity and Scripture from every other religion and philosophy of life.
            a. The Protestant Reformation of the sixteenth century championed anew the truth.
            b. Centuries later, modernists and, today, post-modernists deny this authority and locate the authority in life and all the questions wrapped up in it within humanity.
   B. Joseph Henry Thayer, a nineteenth-century modernist, captured the essence of this modernist movement of autonomy in his work "The Change of Attitude toward the Bible" (1891).
      i. He wrote, "But by reason of improved methods of philological study of progress in science and discovery, of accumulating results and archeological and historical research, the theory of inspiration has come to occasion restlessness and perplexity, at times not a little distress in thoughtful souls. It has become a yoke, which they, unlike their fathers, are unable to bear."
      ii. Thayer, as the quote indicates, advocated higher criticism, a form of literary study of the Bible originating in Germany and popular in the United States beginning in the nineteenth century.
         1. Higher criticism and its proponents denied biblical inspiration and inerrancy in favor of human intellectualism and study.
         2. As biblical inspiration and inerrancy fell away, the theory "newer is better" prevailed and modernists branded the Bible as outdated and not authoritative over modern man.
   C. A fundamental question arises: do we believe the Bible is the Word of God?
      i. To say that the Bible is divinely inspired does not revoke human authorship.
         1. The biblical authors did not enter a trance-like state when they penned Scripture but employed their personalities and wrote in the situation of life in which they moved.
         2. They wrote so that their readers and those who followed might understand.
      ii. Nonetheless, as 2 Timothy 3:16–17 confirms, God inspired and crafted His Word through these writers.

1. The Bible is not simply a thoughtful, stimulating piece of literature.
2. Scripture originates in God, and He uses human instruments for its inscripturation.

D. 2 Peter 1:16–21 reinforces the truth of divine inspiration and human authorship.
   i. The message Peter brought came from God.
   ii. Peter declares that prophecy never originated in man.
   iii. The rest of Scripture sounds this same chord, with Jesus, God incarnate, speaking from His own authority given to Him by His Father.

E. Many views on the doctrine of Scripture exist today, but at least three views remain prevalent.
   i. The liberal view: Scripture is not the Word of God, but it may possess abiding (inspired?) truths.
   ii. A second view professes that the Bible is not the Word of God, but when the Bible is proclaimed, the Lord inspires this proclamation. (Karl Barth championed this view.)
   iii. The verbal plenary view: every word of the Bible is inspired.

STUDY QUESTIONS

1. The word *theopneustos* means ___________.
   a. "God-infused"
   b. "God-spoken"
   c. "God-breathed"
   d. "God-approved"

2. The authority of Scripture comes from "top-down."
   a. True
   b. False

3. Higher criticism upholds biblical inspiration and inerrancy.
   a. True
   b. False

4. Divine inspiration excludes human personality and style in authorship.
   a. True
   b. False

5. Who championed the view that the Word of God is inspired only when it is proclaimed?
   a. Henry Fosdick
   b. Karl Barth
   c. Joseph Henry Thayer
   d. B.B. Warfield

BIBLE STUDY AND DISCUSSION QUESTIONS

1. What does 2 Timothy 3:16–17 say about the origin of Scripture? How does this origination affect the Christian life?

2. How does the authority of Scripture proceed? How does this position differ from every other religion and philosophy for life?

3. Describe the modernist and post-modernist position. How does Joseph Henry Thayer's quote from "The Change of Attitude toward the Bible" epitomize this stance?

4. What is higher criticism? Where did it originate? How and why does it revoke biblical inspiration and inerrancy?

5. Is divine inspiration incompatible with human authorship? Why or why not? List the three views on inspiration given in this lesson.

3

The Authority of Scripture, Part 2—The Doctrine of Inerrancy

MESSAGE INTRODUCTION

For many years, mainline academia has issued attacks against the Bible through the various fields of study, such as history and archaeology. The lack of archaeological evidence supporting Scripture's claims as well as its attestation of supernatural events form just a few of the arrows shot by those seeking to poke holes in the positions of inspiration and inerrancy. Although engagement in these intellectual debates is appropriate and useful, at the end of the day, once all the objections have been leveled and answered, satisfactory to some or not, the most important question must float to the surface and receive response: will human beings submit to the authority of God's inspired, inerrant Word? The answer has eternal ramifications.

SCRIPTURE READINGS

Numbers 23:19; 2 Samuel 7:28; Proverbs 30:5; John 10:35; Romans 10:18–21; 2 Peter 3:16

TEACHING OBJECTIVES

1. To illuminate how Scripture links God's Word with His character
2. To introduce the International Council for Biblical Inerrancy and explain its proclamation on inerrancy
3. To demonstrate Scripture's stance on inerrancy
4. To explain the doctrine of self-attestation

QUOTATION

Nothing, therefore, can be more absurd than the fiction, that the power of judging Scripture is in the church, and that on her nod its certainty depends. When the church receives it, and gives it the stamp of her authority, she does not make that authentic which was otherwise doubtful or controverted but, acknowledging it as the truth of God, she, as in duty bound, shows her reverence by an unhesitating assent. As to the questions, How shall we be persuaded that it came from God without recurring to a decree of the church? it is just the same as if it were asked, How shall we learn to distinguish light from darkness, white from black, sweet from bitter? Scripture bears upon the face of it as clear evidence of its truth, as white and black do of their color, sweet and bitter of their taste.

—an excerpt from John Calvin's *Institutes of the Christian Religion*

LECTURE OUTLINE

I. The Doctrine of Inerrancy
   A. If Scripture is God's Word, as we spoke about in the previous session, the doctrine of inerrancy must follow.
   B. Scripture, as the Word of God, reflects His character.
      i. Numbers 23:19: "God is not man, that he should lie, or a son of man, that he should change his mind. Has he said, and will he not do it? Or has he spoken, and will he not fulfill it?"
      ii. This passage links God's Word with His character, which remains true, reliable, and trustworthy.
      iii. Polycarp, an early church father and bishop of Smyrna, demonstrates the apostolic church's understanding of the veracity of Scripture by quoting it to add credence to his exhortations.
   C. In the 1960's and the decades following, evangelical denominations around the United States wrestled with the inspiration and inerrancy of Scripture.
   D. In response to this struggle within American Protestantism, a group of pastors, theologians, and churchmen convened at Chicago for the International Council for Biblical Inerrancy.
      i. The council consisted of theologians such as R.C. Sproul, J.I. Packer, and James Montgomery Boice.
      ii. The council issued a definitive, nuanced statement of the doctrine of inerrancy.
         1. The council declared that the Bible is a truthful recording of human speech.
            a. The Bible contains phenomenological language (i.e. language used to describe phenomena experienced by a human author).
            b. An example of phenomenological language is the expression "The sun rises." The sun does not actually rise, but we use this language to describe our experience.
         2. The declaration reiterated B.B. Warfield's profession that the origin of the Bible in God necessitates its veracity.
   E. Scripture declares God's Word to be true, and, consequently, Scripture is trustworthy.

- i. Proverbs 30:5: Every word God speaks proves true, and this enables us to flee to Him as a sure refuge.
- ii. 2 Samuel 7:28: God's words are true, and He does not fail to keep His promises.
- iii. Jesus responds to Satan's temptations and lies with Scripture, implicitly proving its truth, and He also claims that Scripture "cannot be broken," demonstrating its veracity (John 10:35).
- iv. Paul uses the Old Testament to provide authority and proof of his argument in Romans 10.
- v. In 2 Peter 3:16, Peter places Paul's epistles on the same level as the Old Testament Scriptures, indicating that they are inspired and inerrant.

F. Theologians speak of the Bible as "self-attesting."
- i. "Self-attestation" refers to the internal testimony of Scripture to its own veracity.
    1. The Reformers referred to this doctrine as *testimonium internum Spiritis Sancti*: "internal testimony of the Holy Spirit."
    2. The Word of God does not derive its authority from the church, but the authority derives from its origin from God. The Holy Spirit persuades God's church of this truth.
    3. External data, such as historical studies and archaeological findings, support the truth of Scripture, but they do not serve as its proof.
- ii. The final and most important question for the doctrine of inspiration and inerrancy involves submission: are we willing to submit to the Word of God or not?

STUDY QUESTIONS

1. Numbers 23:19 links God's Word with His character, which is trustworthy.
    a. True
    b. False

2. Polycarp used Scripture to authorize and prove the exhortations in his letters to churches.
    a. True
    b. False

3. In response to the struggle over biblical inerrancy within American Protestantism, a group of pastors, theologians, and churchmen convened where for the International Council for Biblical Inerrancy?
    a. New York
    b. Philadelphia
    c. Chicago
    d. Los Angeles

4. Phenomenological language is language used to describe phenomena experienced by a human author.
   a. True
   b. False

5. What does *testimonium internum Spiritis Sancti* mean?
   a. "verified testimony"
   b. "internal testimony of the Holy Spirit"
   c. "sanctified testimony"
   d. "secret knowledge of the Holy Spirit"

BIBLE STUDY AND DISCUSSION QUESTIONS

1. Why does Scripture reflect the character of God? How does Scripture reflect the character of God? Read Number 23:19 and explain how this passage provides insight into these questions.

2. Explain how the International Council for Biblical Inerrancy originated. What did the council rule?

3. What is phenomenological language? Does it revoke the veracity of Scripture? Give examples of phenomenological language in Scripture and explain their purpose.

4. How and where does Scripture declare itself to be true and trustworthy?

5. What is self-attestation? What does Dr. Nichols understand as the bottom-line question in debate over biblical inspiration and inerrancy?

4

Why Sixty-Six Books? The Development of the Canon

MESSAGE INTRODUCTION

The past few decades have witnessed a resurgence of criticism against the authority of the canon of Scripture. Books like *The da Vinci Code* seek to undermine the foundations of Christianity by shedding doubt on the cornerstone of its structure: the Word of God. Sadly, these critiques generally invent lies and falsify information to create "persuasive" arguments against the authority of Scripture, and one of the most common areas in which this occurs is the canonization process of the Bible. Yet, as this lesson demonstrates, the early church faced similar problems and struggles as they received God's Word, and the wisdom He granted them to confront these problems and the faithfulness He demonstrated during their time should instruct and encourage us in our own day.

SCRIPTURE READINGS

Joshua 1:8–9; Luke 24:13–49; 1 Corinthians 11:23–26; 2 Peter 3:16

TEACHING OBJECTIVES

1. To explain the difference between Roman Catholicism and Protestantism on the process of canonization
2. To demonstrate how Scripture and the early church affirmed the Old Testament as inspired and authoritative
3. To illuminate the canonization process of the New Testament
4. To demonstrate how Scripture and the early church affirmed the New Testament as inspired and authoritative

QUOTATION

But Hermas wrote The Shepherd very recently, in our times, in the city of Rome, while bishop Pius, his brother, was occupying the chair of the church of the city of Rome. And therefore it ought indeed to be read; but it cannot be read publicly to the people in church either among the Prophets, whose number is complete, or among the Apostles, for it is after their time.

—An excerpt from the Muratorian Fragment

LECTURE OUTLINE

I. The Development of the Canon
  A. The word "canon" derives from the Greek word *kanōn*, meaning "measuring rod, standard."
  B. Protestants and Roman Catholics think differently about the issue of canon.
    i. In Roman Catholicism, the Roman Catholic Church *establishes* the canon.
    ii. Protestants substitute the word "establishes" for the word "recognize."
      1. The process of canonization is the process of the church recognizing which books are canonical and which are not.
      2. The difference between these two positions is substantive.
  C. Scripture establishes the canon of the Old Testament (containing thirty-nine books) internally.
    i. The first section of the Old Testament is the Law, the first five books of the Old Testament (a.k.a Torah or Pentateuch).
      1. Joshua 1:8–9 refers to the Book of the Law as the center of Israel's life.
      2. The prophets refer to the Law in this same manner, constantly pointing back to it and the covenant contained within to instigate Israel to live properly before the Lord.
      3. These passages and others demonstrate the inspiration and authority of the Law.
    ii. Jesus also understands the Old Testament and its components as authoritative.
      1. Jesus quotes from the book of Proverbs, attributing His quotes to God.
      2. On the road to Emmaus, Jesus reveals all that was written about Him in the Old Testament, beginning with Moses and the prophets (Luke 24:13–35).
      3. Jesus reveals Himself to the disciples and explains that "everything written about me in the Law of Moses and the Prophets and the Psalms must be fulfilled" (Luke 24:44).
        a. This passage refers to the three sections of the Hebrew Bible (the Old Testament), the Tanakh.
        b. Tanakh is an abstraction from the three Hebrew words for the three sections of the Hebrew Bible: Torah ("ta"; "law"), Nevi'im ("na"; "prophets"), and Ketuvim ("kh"; "writings").

c. Jesus' and the other New Testament authors' use of these three sections of the Old Testament demonstrates that they are inspired and authoritative.

D. The New Testament does not provide a firm list of the thirty-nine Old Testament books.
   i. Although the Jews recognized the Old Testament and its thirty-nine books as authoritative, the influence of Greek philosophy led some to rescind this authority and remove some, if not all, of the books.
      1. A central tenet of Greek philosophy viewed the physical as inferior to the spiritual, and sometimes even evil.
      2. Marcion (circa AD 150) employed this philosophy when he formed his list of canonical books and rejected the Old Testament.
   ii. Melito, the bishop of Sardis, among many others, denounced Marcion and issued a list of the canon containing the thirty-nine books of the Old Testament, affirming the Jewish tradition of hundreds of years.
E. The canonization of the New Testament featured a different process.
   i. The New Testament authors explicitly verify the inspiration and authority of much of the New Testament.
      1. The epistles of the New Testament quote from the gospels and refer to their content as authoritative (e.g. Paul in 1 Corinthians 11:23–26, in regards to the Lord's Supper).
      2. Peter refers to Paul's epistles as authoritative and on the level of Scripture (2 Peter 3:16).
   ii. The bishops and churchmen of the early church refer to much of Scripture as authoritative in their own writings and communications (e.g. Polycarp of Smyrna).
   iii. By roughly AD 100, the four gospels, the letters of Paul, Acts, and some of the general epistles are recognized as canonical—around eighty-five percent of the New Testament we have today.
   iv. Outside of this eighty-five percent, a number of works existed that did not receive universal acceptance but still existed and circulated in the ancient church.
      1. Works like the Gospel of Judas and the Apocalypse of Peter, originating in the second century and beyond, circulated at this time.
      2. Some, like Bart Ehrman, believe that their presence legitimates their place as canonical and authoritative.
      3. This reasoning is unfair to the data, as it denounces the particular orthodox view from the ancient time period by virtue of its preeminence alone.
   v. The Muratorian Fragment, discovered by Ludovico Antonio Muratori, sheds light on the process of canonization in the early church.
      1. The fragment demonstrates that the church used three criteria for recognizing a canonical work.

   a. The book had to be written by an apostle.
      1) Apostles were eyewitnesses, an important feature of legitimate testimony in the ancient world.
      2) Apostles had an authority of office and spoke from God.
      3) The Muratorian Fragment mentions the work *The Shepherd of Hermas*, probably written by Hermas. It commends the work, but it does not attribute authority to it because Hermas was not an apostle.
   b. The book must have appropriate theological content.
      1) The book must not contradict other Scripture.
      2) The Fragment renounces many Gnostic works, similar to the Gospel of Judas, for its contradictory message.
   c. The work must be accepted by the church.
      1) The church receives the work. It does not establish it.
      2) The church must view the book as canonical.

F. In AD 367, Athanasius, bishop of Alexandria, writes a letter confirming the twenty-seven books of the New Testament, and in AD 397, the Synod of Carthage convenes and agrees to the list of Athanasius for the New Testament and reaffirms Melito's list of the Old Testament.

STUDY QUESTIONS

1. What does the Greek word *kanōn* mean?
   a. "cannon"
   b. "dignified"
   c. "testimony"
   d. "measuring rod"

2. What are the three sections of the Old Testament?
   a. Law, Epistles, Writings
   b. Creation, Law, Prophets
   c. Law, Prophets, Writings
   d. Law, Prophets, Apocalypse

3. The early church sided with Marcion and his canonical list over and above Melito.
   a. True
   b. False

4. The Muratorian Fragment supported *The Shepherd of Hermas* as a canonical work.
   a. True
   b. False

5. The Council of Carthage was the first council of the church to confirm officially the entire biblical corpus.
   a. True
   b. False

BIBLE STUDY AND DISCUSSION QUESTIONS

1. How do Roman Catholics and Protestants think differently about the process of canonization?

2. How does the New Testament legitimize the authority of the Old Testament already known and accepted by the Jews for centuries? Why did some in the early church discredit this authority, and how did the church respond?

3. How does the New Testament explicitly testify to its own authority? What other support exists in the early church for the authority of Scripture? Roughly how much of Scripture was seen as canonical circa AD 100?

4. Why do some, like Bart Ehrman, want to legitimize all the ancient works claiming authority in the early church? Why is this unfair?

5. What is the Muratorian Fragment? What criteria does it list for a canonical work?

5

Why So Many Interpretations? The Clarity of Scripture & Interpretation

MESSAGE INTRODUCTION

You may hear people in certain circles of evangelicalism claim that they do not need teachers or instructors of Scripture, for, as Jeremiah says, "And no longer shall each one teach his neighbor and each his brother, saying, 'Know the LORD,' for they shall all know me, from the least of them to the greatest, declares the LORD. For I will forgive their iniquity, and I will remember their sin no more" (Jer. 31:34). The New Testament affirms Jeremiah's message, and it explains that the fundamental message of the gospel is clear and easy to understand if the Holy Spirit enables the heart. However, as Peter declares in his second epistle, clarity does not equal simplicity—as Paul's epistles frequently remind us. Understanding and interpreting Scripture requires the illumination of Scripture, a heart for the Lord, and discipline, as Dr. Nichols reveals to us in this lesson.

SCRIPTURE READINGS

Isaiah 64:4; John 14:16–18; 15:26–27; 16:7–15; 1 Corinthians 2

TEACHING OBJECTIVES

1. To explain the process of illumination and the Holy Spirit's role in it
2. To demonstrate the clarity of Scripture while revoking the idea that it is simple
3. To discuss why there are many interpretations of Scripture and to provide seven ways to interpret it

QUOTATION

Your words were found, and I ate them,
and your words became to me a joy
and the delight of my heart,
for I am called by your name,
O LORD, God of hosts.

—Jeremiah 15:16

LECTURE OUTLINE

I. The Clarity of Scripture
   A. The Reformers understood the necessity of clarity in Scripture in order for it to be authoritative.
      i. Just as the Holy Spirit inspired the biblical authors, the Spirit illuminates the minds of believers to understand the Word.
      ii. John 14–16 explains this role of the Spirit.
         1. The Reformers referred to the Spirit as *Magister Veritatis,* the "teacher of truth," based on Christ's words in these passages.
         2. The disciples were troubled because Jesus had reiterated His imminent departure.
         3. Jesus allays their fears by reaffirming that they will meet again and also telling them that when He leaves, He will send them the Comforter who will lead them into truth. This is the ministry of the Holy Spirit.
         4. The Spirit fulfilled Jesus' words by bringing to the minds of the Apostles the works and sayings of Jesus so that they might inscripturate them.
      iii. Paul explains in 1 Corinthians 2 how the Spirit also fulfills Jesus' words by revealing to the minds of believers the truth of God's Word.
         1. Quoting from Isaiah 64:4, Paul declares that the Spirit alone, the teacher of truth, illuminates to man the message of Scripture.
         2. Despite this ministry of truth, differences of interpretation and understanding still exist among the church.
   B. Although Scripture is clear, this does not mean that it is simple.
      i. Any man can read Scripture and understand the basic message of the gospel: repent of your sins and believe in Jesus, the incarnated Son of God, for your salvation.
         1. This message of the gospel is clear.
         2. Other aspects of the Word of God, however, are not so easy to understand, such as the nature of the God-man.
      ii. However, true illumination and, consequently, clarity occur only when the Holy Spirit enables an individual to embrace the message of salvation with his whole being.

1. The Bible frequently refers to this illumination as a difference between darkness and light: an individual persists in darkness until the Spirit brings him into the light so that he might see.
2. The Spirit does not add anything to Scripture but just enables true sight of what already exists.

C. Many interpretations of Scripture exist due to the nature of Scripture and the nature of humanity.
   i. Human beings enter into the study of Scripture as fallen creatures with presuppositions and experiences that cultivate and dictate their understandings.
   ii. Scripture should serve to control and correct our understanding, but when we enforce our perspective, we fail to allow Scripture to inform us, but we inform it.
   iii. Seven ways to interpret Scripture
      1. Read the Bible reverently.
      2. Read the Bible prayerfully.
      3. Read the Bible collectively.
      4. Read the Bible humbly.
      5. Read the Bible carefully.
         a. A careful interpretation of the Bible involves the application of historical, grammatical, cultural, rhetorical, and theological methodology.
         b. Context serves as an important component of interpretation.
      6. Read the Bible Christologically.
         a. Everything in the Word points to Christ.
         b. Interpretation should seek to understand the function of each passage in relation to its ultimate goal: to reveal the Savior.
      7. Read the Bible obediently.

STUDY QUESTIONS

1. The second Person of the Trinity, the Son, plays the important role of illumination in the heart of believers.
   a. True
   b. False

2. The Reformers applied the title *Magister Veritatis* to whom?
   a. The Holy Spirit
   b. The Father
   c. The Son
   d. The Apostle Paul

3. Any man may read Scripture and choose to embrace it without any divine assistance.
   a. True
   b. False

4. Scripture should serve to correct and control our understanding and interpretation of it.
   a. True
   b. False

5. Everything in Scripture leads us to ___________.
   a. Jesus Christ
   b. the glory of man
   c. the end of times
   d. the aseity of God

BIBLE STUDY AND DISCUSSION QUESTIONS

1. What does John 14–16 reveal about the role of the Holy Spirit in illumination?

2. How does the Holy Spirit fulfill His role according to Paul in 1 Corinthians 2?

3. Is Scripture clear? Why or why not? Is Scripture simple? Why or why not? Support your answers with Scripture.

4. How does an individual embrace the truths of Scripture? Why do many interpretations of Scripture exist?

5. List and explain Nichols' seven ways to interpret Scripture.

6

Scripture for Life— The Sufficiency of Scripture

MESSAGE INTRODUCTION

The concept that an ancient book might offer sufficiency for life rubs against the grain of our postmodern culture. How can one source possess all the answers for life, let alone an archaic, outdated text? Behind this question lies the desire for the individual to choose what is sufficient, a grasp for autonomy that began with our first parents in the garden of Eden. They sought to cast off the yoke of the Lord, which they considered heavy and unnecessary, and instead they exalted themselves to the place of their Creator, arbiters of sufficiency. This sin remains alive today, compelling Christians who have tasted the streams of everlasting life flowing from our Savior to proclaim the truth that life and its rule may only be found in Christ and His Word.

SCRIPTURE READINGS

Isaiah 40:6–8; 1 Peter 1:22–25; 2 Peter 1:3–4a

TEACHING OBJECTIVES

1. To define the sufficiency of Scripture and the place it has in the Christian life
2. To illuminate through Scripture the precious gift of its sufficiency and the need to proclaim this sufficiency to all the nations

QUOTATION

The whole counsel of God concerning all things necessary for His own glory, man's salvation, faith and life, is either expressly set down in Scripture, or by good and necessary consequence may be deduced from Scripture: unto which nothing at any time is to be added, whether by new revelations of the Spirit, or traditions of men. Nevertheless, we acknowledge the inward illumination of the Spirit of God to be necessary for the saving understanding of such things as are revealed in the Word: and that there are some circumstances concerning the worship of God, and government of the Church, common to human actions and societies, which are to be ordered by the light of nature, and Christian prudence, according to the general rules of the Word, which are always to be observed.

—Westminster Confession of Faith I.VI.

LECTURE OUTLINE

I. The Sufficiency of Scripture
   A. In our last lesson, Dr. Nichols explained that we must read Scripture obediently and allow it to act as a mirror for our life. This truth results from the assumption that Scripture is a sufficient guide for life.
   B. Not everyone shares this assumption about Scripture.
      i. Modernity views the Bible as ancient and outdated, unable to measure up against scientific standards and insufficient for life.
      ii. Postmodernity remains suspicious of the Bible because it claims to provide answers for life and to serve as the only source of these answers, concepts irreconcilable and unrealistic to this worldview. It prefers a plurality of voices.
      iii. Although these worldviews clash with a biblical worldview, they have the potential to seep into our orthodox stance unwittingly and subtly.
   C. Although Scripture is sufficient for all of life (e.g. parenting, financial management), it is not exhaustive (i.e. it does not provide instructions for every activity in life, but it does provide principles for every area and aspect of life).
      i. 2 Peter 1:3–4a states, "His divine power has granted to us all things that pertain to life and godliness, through the knowledge of him who called us to his own glory and excellence, by which he has granted to us his precious and very great promises, so that through them you may become partakers of the divine nature."
         1. This passage declares the sufficiency of Scripture for the Christian life.
         2. Peter refers to the promises of God as *precious*, and his language demonstrates the importance and value of God's Word and the life it grants.
      ii. 1 Peter 1:22–25 states, "Having purified your souls by your obedience to the truth for a sincere brotherly love, love one another earnestly from a pure heart, since you have been born again, not of perishable seed but of imperishable, through the living and abiding word of God; for 'All flesh is like grass and all its glory like the flower of grass. The grass withers, and the flower falls, but the word of the Lord remains forever.' And this word is the good news that was preached to you."
         1. Peter uses as the main verb in this section "to love one another," indicating that loving one another with a pure, sincere heart is of the utmost importance for the Christian life.
         2. How do we attain this pure heart? We attain this pure heart only through the sufficient, living Word of God.

   a. This Word of God is living and imperishable, in contrast to the many worldly voices that attempt to clamor over it.
   b. This Word alone may claim the title of "good news."
3. Peter's use of Isaiah recalls the imagery of God as the Shepherd leading His people Israel back from the Babylonian exile through harsh conditions to the Promised Land. The Lord's strength is sufficient to provide for His people, a strength He delivers through His Word.
4. Peter also had in mind, from Isaiah, the need to preach the good news, so that others might learn about their need for the Lord and the saving grace and sufficiency found in His Word.

STUDY QUESTIONS

1. Reading Scripture obediently results from the assumption that Scripture is sufficient for all of life.
   a. True
   b. False

2. Modernity and postmodernity accept the sufficiency of Scripture and should be embraced by a Christian worldview.
   a. True
   b. False

3. Scripture is sufficient for all of life as well as exhaustive for all of life.
   a. True
   b. False

4. The main verb in 1 Peter 1:22–25 is __________.
   a. "to love one another"
   b. "preached"
   c. "having purified"
   d. "having been born again"

5. Peter quotes from which book of the Bible in the first chapter of his first epistle?
   a. Jeremiah
   b. Ezekiel
   c. Daniel
   d. Isaiah

BIBLE STUDY AND DISCUSSION QUESTIONS

1. What is the assumption underlying an obedient reading of Scripture? Why?

2. How do modernity and postmodernity view the doctrine of the sufficiency of Scripture? How should Christians view and utilize the tools that modernity and postmodernity make ultimate in their search and explanation of life?

3. Is Scripture exhaustive for all of life? Why or why not? What does 2 Peter 1:3–4a say on the subject of the sufficiency of Scripture and the promises that God gives?

4. What is Peter's main desire for the Christian life as expressed in 1 Peter 1:22–25? How can Christians do this?

5. What differentiates the Word of God from all the other competing worldviews that have arisen, arise today, and will arise tomorrow? How does the truth of this revelation and the competition of false worldviews encourage the Christian to proclaim the good news?